Searchlight BOOKS™

The World of Gaming

# The World of Mario Bros.

**Buffy Silverman**

**Lerner Publications ◆ Minneapolis**

Lerner Publications Company
A division of Lerner Publishing Group, Inc.
241 First Avenue North
Minneapolis, MN 55401 USA

For reading levels and more information, look up this title
at www.lernerbooks.com.

**Library of Congress Cataloging-in-Publication Data**

The Cataloging-in-Publication Data for *The World of Mario Bros.* is on file at the Library
  of Congress.
ISBN 978-1-5124-8315-4 (lib. bdg.)
ISBN 978-1-5415-1197-2 (pbk.)
ISBN 978-1-5124-8311-6 (EB pdf)

Manufactured in the United States of America
1-43328-33148-9/21/2017

# Contents

# Chapter 1

# FROM JUMPMAN TO MARIO

You press a button and Mario races across a brick platform. He nears an enemy Goomba, a small mushroom-like creature. You tap another button and Mario jumps. He lands on the Goomba and flattens it.

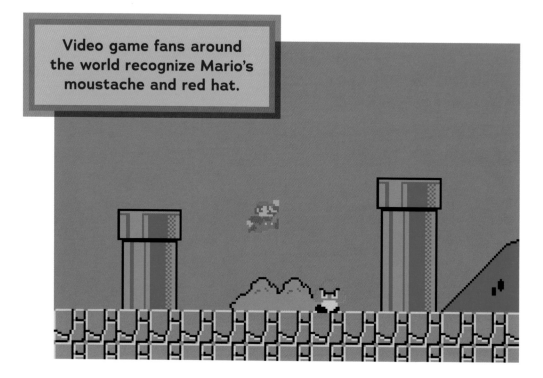

**Video game fans around the world recognize Mario's moustache and red hat.**

Mario is one of the world's most popular video game characters. But he wasn't always the star of his own game. He first appeared in 1981 in an arcade game called *Donkey Kong*. You put coins in an arcade machine to start a game.

When *Donkey Kong* was designed by the Japanese company Nintendo, Mario was called Jumpman. He was named for his favorite move. He jumped over barrels and from one platform to another.

Before the game was released, Nintendo employees met in a warehouse in the United States to view the new game. They thought Jumpman needed a different name. During their meeting, the owner of the warehouse arrived. His name was Mario. Soon Jumpman was named Mario too!

Donkey Kong has a never-ending supply of barrels to throw at Mario.

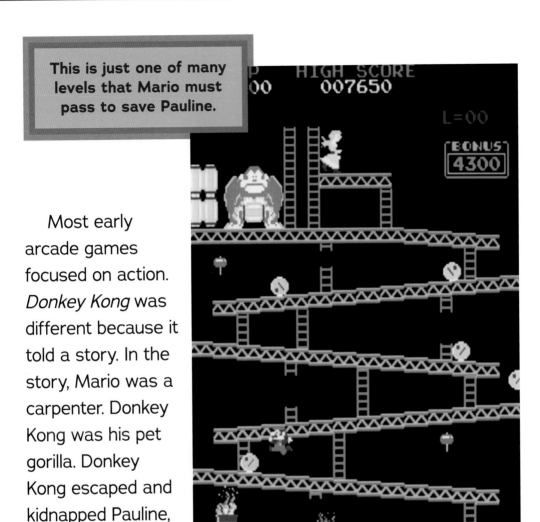

Most early arcade games focused on action. *Donkey Kong* was different because it told a story. In the story, Mario was a carpenter. Donkey Kong was his pet gorilla. Donkey Kong escaped and kidnapped Pauline, Mario's girlfriend. The gorilla carried Pauline off to a construction site.

When you played the game, you took the role of Mario. You climbed platforms and ladders. Donkey Kong threw barrels and fireballs at you. You leaped over them and tried to rescue Pauline.

7

# Meet Shigeru Miyamoto

Did you know that the man who created Mario is one of the world's most famous video game designers? When Shigeru Miyamoto was a boy, he made puppets and drew comics. He wanted to be a manga artist. Manga is a style of comic book from Japan.

After college, Miyamoto became a designer at Nintendo. When Nintendo needed a new video game, they asked Miyamoto to write and design it. He thought about the comic book stories that he had loved as a boy. He wanted to make video games that would bring stories to life. That's why he created *Donkey Kong* and *Super Mario Bros.* Since then, he's made many more games. Mario stars in most of them.

## Mario and Luigi

In 1983, Mario starred in an arcade game called *Mario Bros.* The game took place in the sewers under New York City. The game designers changed Mario from a carpenter to a plumber because of all the pipes.

Two people can play *Mario Bros.* at the same time. One player acts as Mario, and the other takes the role of his brother, Luigi. Mario and Luigi fight enemies that invade the sewers.

*Mario Bros.* wasn't as popular as *Donkey Kong*. But the *Mario Bros.* sequel became one of the best-selling video games of all time. *Super Mario Bros.* sold more than forty million copies. Many more Mario games followed.

PEOPLE PLAYED *SUPER MARIO BROS.* ON THE NINTENDO ENTERTAINMENT SYSTEM.

# Chapter 2

# SAVE THE PRINCESS, FREE THE KINGDOM

In 1985, *Super Mario Bros.* became a smash hit. The game's story takes place in Mushroom Kingdom. Princess Peach and her father, the Mushroom King, rule the Mushroom People. Evil turtles called Koopa invade the kingdom. They are led by Bowser, a powerful turtle with horns and claws.

The Koopa use dark magic to turn Mushroom People into rocks and bricks. Only Princess Peach can break the spell and save her people. But Bowser captures the princess. Mario sets out to save Princess Peach and the Mushroom People.

**Bowser has been appearing in Mario games for more than thirty years.**

As Mario, you travel through eight different worlds to free the princess. Each world has four levels. You reach the end of a level by jumping gaps, running across platforms, and bouncing on boards. Pipes lead to secret rooms filled with coins.

MARIO
017850        ) x 21

WORLD
1-2

TIME
310

A level ends when
Mario takes down
the enemy flag.

2000

# Meet a Video Game Writer

Do you like to make up stories? Then you might want to be a video game writer! A video game writer is part of a team that develops a game's story.

A writer researches background material. For example, if a game takes place during another time, the writer learns how characters lived and dressed at that time. A writer decides how best to tell the story and create the characters.

A video game writer may write a script for actors who play the characters in a game.

# Defeat the Enemy!

Many enemies appear in Mario's path. Koopa Troopas and Buzzy Beetles attack him. But they hide in their shells when Mario jumps on them. Piranha Plants try to bite Mario. He shoots fireballs or kicks turtle shells at them. He shoots fireballs at underwater Bloopers and Cheep Cheeps.

Piranha Plants (*left*) and Koopa Troopas (*right*) are easy to avoid at first. They get faster and more active as the game proceeds.

When the game begins, Mario is his usual size. He touches a Super Mushroom to grow into Super Mario. Super Mario has special powers. He doesn't lose a life if an enemy hits him. Instead, he shrinks back to normal. Mario can break blocks only when he is Super Mario. A player gets points for breaking blocks.

Mario (*left*) can turn into Super Mario (*right*).

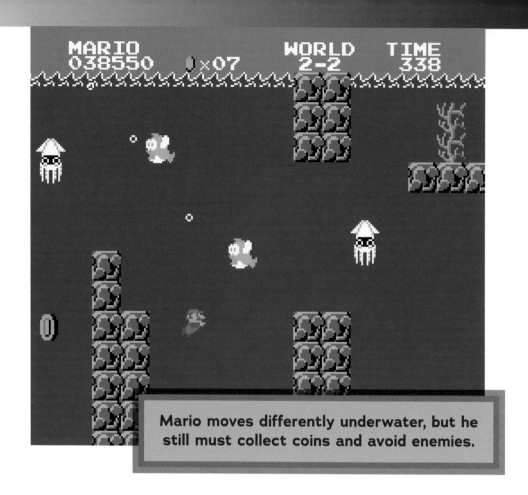

MARIO 038550 ⓞ×07 WORLD 2-2 TIME 338

Mario moves differently underwater, but he still must collect coins and avoid enemies.

*Donkey Kong* is a single-screen platform game. Characters run on platforms, ledges, or stairs. The action occurs on a single screen and doesn't change until the player completes a level.

*Super Mario Bros.* is a side-scrolling platform game. It takes place in many different settings. Mario moves from the left side of the screen to the right side. The background changes as he moves through Mushroom Kingdom. *Super Mario Bros.* made side-scrolling platform games popular.

# Chapter 3

# MARIO MANIA

People around the world recognize Mario. The plumber dressed in overalls appears in more than two hundred video games that have sold more than five hundred million copies. He lives beyond video games too. You can buy Mario T-shirts, mugs, and lunch boxes. You can collect Mario toys and wear Mario jewelry. You can listen to albums of music from Mario video games.

**Mario gear is a popular way for fans to show off their love for the character.**

Mario stars in several manga series. *Super Mario-Kun* is one of the most popular Mario comics. Japanese children have read this monthly series for more than twenty-five years.

The comics are also translated into English and other languages. They feature Mario and more characters from the video games. Some of the stories are based on the games. Others are found only in comic books. The manga also feature Mario puzzles for readers to solve.

**Mario fans had a good time at a manga fair in Barcelona, Spain.**

The Super Mario Super Bros. Super Show! aired in 1989.

## Mario at the Movies (and More!)

Mario is the star of several television shows and films. At least twelve television series since 1983 have featured Mario. Many were cartoons called anime. Anime is a colorful style of Japanese animation.

The Super Mario Super Bros. Super Show! included both live-action segments and cartoons. In the show, Mario and Luigi live in Brooklyn. They are sucked down a bathtub drain. The brothers end up in Mushroom Kingdom. There they try to rescue the princess and stop King Bowser.

This Ain't No Game.

S U P E R
MARIO BROS.

Mario and Luigi travel
to another dimension
to battle King Koopa in
*Super Mario Bros.*

Mario movies are also popular. Some star human actors on-screen, such as the 1993 film *Super Mario Bros.* Other movies are anime.

Some Mario anime are based on well-known fairy tales. In one story, Princess Peach plays the role of Snow White. She lives in a forest with seven toads. Jealous Queen Koopa visits Peach when the toads are away. Queen Koopa gives Peach a poisoned apple that puts her in a deep sleep. Mario finds a magic potion to save her. He and Luigi defeat Queen Koopa so she can no longer harm the princess.

# Meet an Animator

Who draws the characters and background in a video game? An animator! An animator uses special software to bring characters to life. The software can make them walk, run, and jump. Animators also draw other moving objects, such as swaying flowers and blowing clouds.

Animators study art and design and have strong computer skills.

Many fans attend conventions with people who share their interest in Mario and other anime characters. Fans wear costumes at the conventions. They go to Mario parties and act out scenes from the games. The prime minister (leader) of Japan is a Mario fan too. He wore a Mario costume at the 2016 Olympic Games in Rio de Janeiro, Brazil!

Dressing up as a game character is called cosplay. It's a combination of the words *costume* and *play*.

# Chapter 4

# MODERN MARIO

*Super Mario Bros.* turned thirty years old in 2015.
Nintendo released *Super Mario Maker* to celebrate.
*Super Mario Maker* lets players create the game. Players
choose where to place coins, bricks, mushrooms, and
enemies. They select settings for the game such as
underground, underwater, or other themes.

 *Super Mario Maker* lets you switch between editing
and playing. You can create part of a level and test it.
Then you can share your level with a friend.

By 2016, players had made more than seven million levels with *Super Mario Maker*!

In *Super Mario Maker*, you can make your level as easy or as difficult as you like.

Shigeru Miyamoto thinks that people love Mario games because players can be creative. *Super Mario Maker* allows players to be more creative than ever before. They decide how they want their game to look and how it will be played. They can experiment and see what happens on their screens.

# Exploring New Worlds

In 2017, Nintendo developed a new adventure for Mario. *Super Mario Odyssey*'s setting is not the Mushroom Kingdom, unlike most other Mario games. Mario's adventures take place in a more realistic-looking world. He grabs onto ledges and jumps off walls in New Donk City. It is modeled on New York City. He also explores deserts and forests.

**Mario has brand-new moves in *Super Mario Odyssey*.**

Most Mario games follow a fixed course. Mario moves through each level from beginning to end. In *Super Mario Odyssey*, a player chooses where Mario will go and what to explore.

Fans play *Super Mario Odyssey* on the Nintendo Switch console. The Switch connects to a television. But the console also has a handheld tablet. You can start a game when you're on the go and then plug it into your TV at home.

**Stores sold out of the Switch quickly when the new console launched in March 2017.**

# Meet a Game Developer

Would you like to make your own video games? That's what game developers do! They create software that runs a game. Game developers test their software to make sure it works correctly. It often takes a team of game developers to write the software for a single game. Some software animates characters on a screen. Other developers create software that controls when different sounds will play.

Mario also has adventures on smartphones. Mario constantly runs forward in *Super Mario Run*. Tap your screen, and he jumps over gaps, onto enemies, and collects coins. You can race against other players and build your own kingdom.

Mario games have changed a lot over the years. They've moved from huge arcade screens to devices that fit in your pocket. Mario will be racing through Mushroom Kingdom for many years to come!

**Like many phone games, you can play *Super Mario Run* with one hand.**

# Bonus Points

- Why does Mario wear a hat? In the 1980s, video game graphics couldn't show much detail. They weren't able to show Mario's hair moving as he ran. Instead, animators gave him a hat.

- How popular is Mario? A survey of children in the United States in the 1990s found that more kids recognized Mario than Mickey Mouse!

- *Super Mario Bros.* was originally supposed to be an action game. Mario would carry a gun and would ride a rocket or a cloud when he was shooting. But the game creators decided to focus on Mario's jumping action instead of shooting.

# Glossary

**anime:** a style of Japanese cartoon

**character:** a person or creature that plays a part in a story

**console:** a device that connects to a TV and plays video games

**convention:** a meeting where people gather to learn more about a common interest

**design:** create something according to a plan

**manga:** Japanese graphic novels or comic books

**platform:** a raised flat surface

**side-scrolling:** a video game where the characters move from the left side of the screen to the right side

**software:** instructions a computer follows to operate

# Learn More about Video Games

## Books

Cornell, Kari. *Nintendo Video Game Designer Shigeru Miyamoto.* Minneapolis: Lerner Publications, 2016. Learn more about the man who made Mario in this fun biography.

Suen, Anastasia. *Alternate Reality Game Designer Jane McGonigal.* Minneapolis: Lerner Publications, 2014. Read all about the life of Jane McGonigal, a designer who makes a different kind of video game.

Woodcock, Jon. *Coding Games in Scratch: A Step-by-Step Visual Guide to Building Your Own Computer Games.* New York: DK, 2016. Knowing how to code is important if you want to create video games, and you can start with this book.

## Websites

How to Draw Super Mario
http://theartspider.com/2017/02/23/draw-super-mario
Watch a video to learn how to draw Mario like a pro.

Mario Facts for Kids
http://wiki.kidzsearch.com/wiki/Mario
Are you looking for even more facts about Mario? This website has what you need.

Nintendo's Official Home for Mario
http://mario.nintendo.com
The official Mario website has everything a Mario fan could want.

# Index

# Photo Acknowledgments

Image acknowledgements: Super Mario Bros, pp. 4, 12, 16; ArcadeImages/Alamy Stock Photo, pp. 5, 7, 9; iStock.com/ilbusca, p. 6; AP Photo/Casey Curry/Invision, p. 8; iStock.com/robtek, p. 10; Nicescene/Shutterstock.com, p. 11; PIUS UTOMI EKPEI/AFP/Getty Images, p. 13; © Harsh Agrawal/flickr.com (CC BY 2.0), p. 14; © Ben Sutherland/flickr.com (CC BY 2.0), p. 15; enchanted_fairy/Shutterstock.com, p. 17; Campillo Rafae/Alamy Stock Photo, p. 18; © DiC Enterprises/Courtesy Everett Collection, p. 19; AF archive/Alamy Stock Photo, p. 20; GUILLERMO LEGARIA/AFP/Getty Images, p. 21; Jose Gil/Shutterstock.com, p. 22; Campillo Rafael/Alamy Stock Photo, p. 23; FREDERIC J. BROWN/AFP/Getty Images, p. 24; Michael Kovac/Getty Images, p. 25; leungchopan/Shutterstock.com, p. 26; iStock.com/Geber86, p. 27; ThomasDeco/Shutterstock.com, p. 28.

Front cover: m.bonotto/Shutterstock.com.

Main body text set in Adrianna Regular 14/20.
Typeface provided by Chank.